What Was It Like Before Television?

Acknowledgments
Executive Editor: Diane Sharpe
Supervising Editor: Stephanie Muller
Design Manager: Sharon Golden
Page Design: Ian Winton
Photography: The Advertising Archives: page 7 (both); Aquarius
Library: page 21 (bottom); The Bettman Archive: page 19; E.T. Archive:
cover (bottom left), page 8; Mary Evans: pages 25, 26; The Hulton Deutsch
Collection: page 21 (top); Mander and Mitchenson: page 23; Alex Ramsay:
cover (middle right), pages 10, 13; Topham Picture Source: page 16.

Library of Congress Cataloging-in-Publication Data
Hankin, Rosie.
    What was it like before television?/Rosie Hankin; illustrated by Diana Bowles.
       p.   cm. — (Read all about it)
    Includes index.
    ISBN 0-8114-5735-4 Hardcover
    ISBN 0-8114-3788-4 Softcover
    1. Amusements — History — Juvenile literature.   2. Games. — History — Juvenile literature.
3. Hobbies — History — Juvenile literature. [1. Amusements. 2. Games 3. Hobbies.] I. Bowles,
Diana, ill. II. Title. III. Series: Read all about it (Austin, Tex.)
GV1200.H34 1995
793'.09—dc20

          94-28574
          CIP
          AC

1 2 3 4 5 6 7 8 9 0 PO 00 99 98 97 96 95 94

STECK-VAUGHN
READ ALL ABOUT IT

What Was It Like Before Television?

Rosie Hankin

Illustrated by
Diana Bowles

STECK-VAUGHN
C O M P A N Y
ELEMENTARY • SECONDARY • ADULT • LIBRARY

We used to make up plays when I was young. There was no television to watch in those days.

> It must have been boring without television.

That is not true! Children had many things
to do before television was invented. Look
at all these old toys and games.

6

Mrs. Brown, tell us about the games you played when you were a child!

7

Before television was invented, people played many board games and card games.

What is this game?

8

My sisters had a stamp collection and a coin collection when they were children.

Look, these stamps are beautiful! They came from France.

My sisters used steam to get stamps off postcards and envelopes. My father always helped them do it.

12

I loved collecting photos, pretty pictures,
and postcards to glue in my scrapbook.
My mother made glue for me out of flour
and water.

My mother taught me how to sew. I also learned how to crochet and embroider.

We played outside on most afternoons.
Sometimes we even made our own toys.

16

We loved making paper kites like these to fly on windy days.

I'm going to fly my kite outside when it's ready.

The roads were safer when I was young because there were very few cars. We used to play in the street with our friends.

Let's play hopscotch.

We will need some chalk to draw on the sidewalk.

18

Sometimes our parents took us to the movie theater. We always saw two movies.

20

Now we can watch movies on television at home.

22

For a special treat, our parents took us to see a funny show. We laughed at all the actors and sang along with all the songs.

I tried to remember the songs so I could sing them when I got home.

I used to play the piano, and my brother played the violin. We often played together.

My mother played the piano, too. Sometimes she would play and sing to us.

25

We listened to the news on the radio. There were special programs for children, too.

We like listening to tapes that tell stories.

My father always read us a book before we went to sleep.

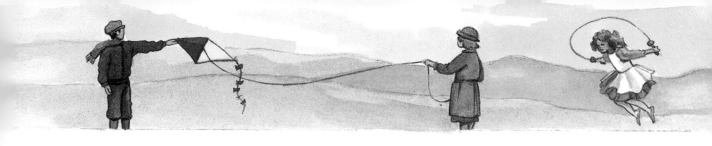

We had so much fun when I was a child. We couldn't watch television, but there were many other fun things to do.

29

The children on this page are very busy.
Do you know what they are doing?
The answers are on the last page, but don't
look until you have tried naming everything.

1.

4.

5.

2.

3.

Index

Answers: 1. Listening to the radio 2. Collecting stamps 3. Playing the violin
4. Making a scrapbook 5. Playing checkers